Making a Difference from HOME

by Hermione Redshaw

Minneapolis, Minnesota

Credits: All images courtesy of Shutterstock.com. With thanks to Getty Images, Thinkstock Photo, and iStockphoto. Front Cover © GoodStudio, AnastasiaNi, Mari Dambi, GoodStudio. 4&5 © Evgeny Atamanenko, AnnaStills. 6&7 © Roman Mikhailiuk, Chernyshkova Natalia, photka. 8&9 © Waridsara_HappyChildren, Evdokimov Maxim. 10&11 © Alrandir, Elena Chevalier. 12&13 © iva, Shyntartanya. 14&15 © Veja, Ruslana Iurchenko. 16&17 © chuchiko17, Akhmad Dody Firmansyah. 18&19 © Southworks, Mashka, Devenorr, TukangPhotoStock, VanderWolf Images, only_kim, fokke baarssen, SkyPics Studio. 20&21 © A3pfamily, Viktor Kochetkov, Marish. 22&23 © AlexandrMusuc, Slavica Stajic, Alfmaler. Title font © Wewhitelist.

Library of Congress Cataloging-in-Publication Data is available at www.loc.gov or upon request from the publisher.

ISBN: 979-8-88509-359-0 (hardcover)
ISBN: 979-8-88509-481-8 (paperback)
ISBN: 979-8-88509-596-9 (ebook)

© 2023 Booklife Publishing
This edition is published by arrangement with Booklife Publishing.

North American adaptations © 2023 Bearport Publishing Company. All rights reserved. No part of this publication may be reproduced in whole or in part, stored in any retrieval system, or transmitted in any form or by any means, electronic, mechanical, photocopying, recording, or otherwise, without written permission from the publisher.

For more information, write to Bearport Publishing, 5357 Penn Avenue South, Minneapolis, MN 55419.

CONTENTS

Our Home 4
Reduce Waste 6
Recycle 8
New from Old 10
Get Creative with Gifts 12
Fix and Reuse 14
Donate It 16
Save Energy 18
Meat-Free Meals 20
Cooking Time 22
Glossary 24
Index 24

OUR HOME

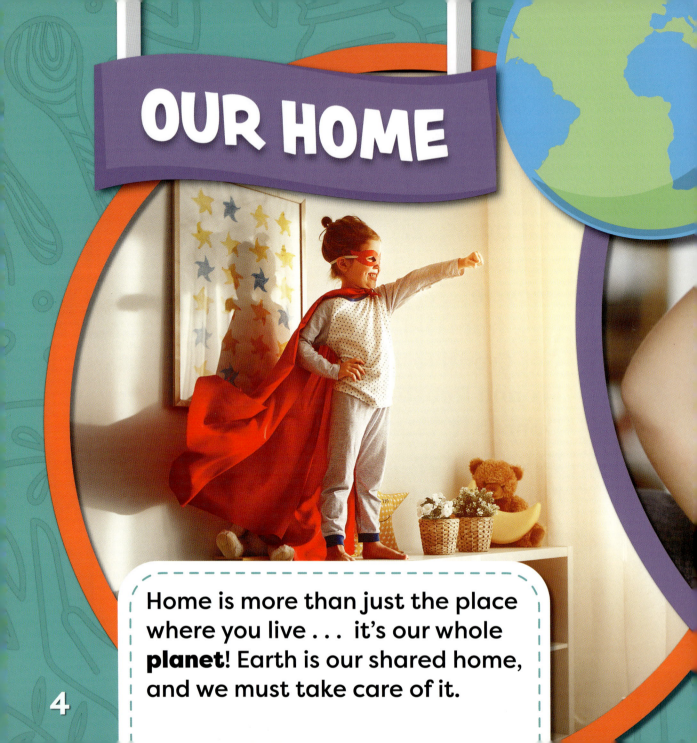

Home is more than just the place where you live . . . it's our whole **planet**! Earth is our shared home, and we must take care of it.

There are many things you can do from your own home to help Earth. You can make a difference. Let's go save the world at home!

About 8 billion people live on Earth.

REDUCE WASTE

One way to help Earth is to make less trash. Most trash goes to **landfills**. The trash piles up, which is bad for our planet.

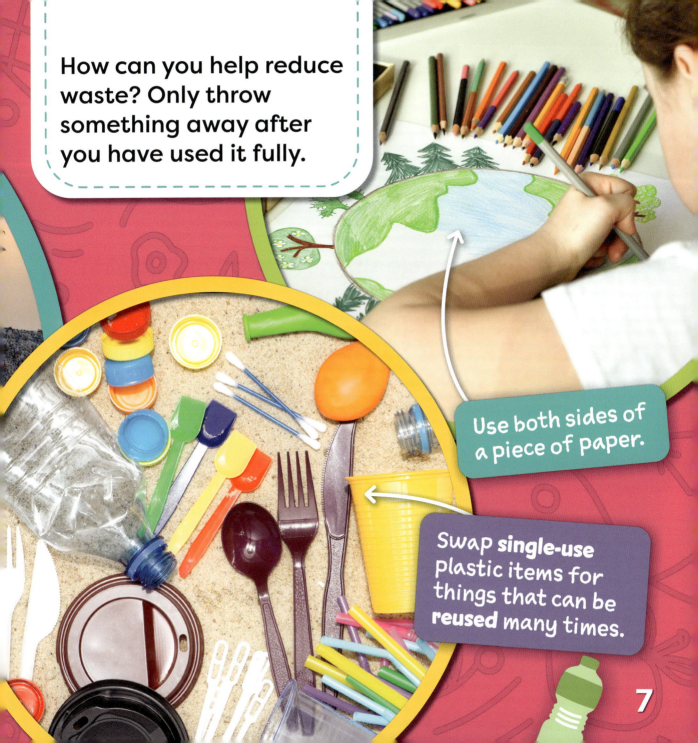

How can you help reduce waste? Only throw something away after you have used it fully.

Use both sides of a piece of paper.

Swap **single-use** plastic items for things that can be **reused** many times.

RECYCLE

You can also **recycle** things instead of throwing them in the trash. This is better for Earth. For example, paper comes from trees. When we recycle paper, fewer trees need to be cut down.

Many people have recycling bins at home. They may recycle these things . . .

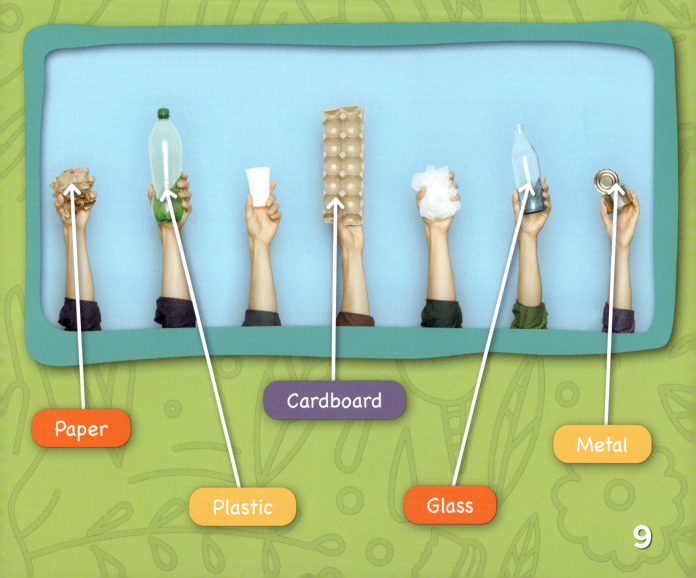

Paper

Plastic

Cardboard

Glass

Metal

NEW FROM OLD

Another way to reduce waste is to make something new from old things around your home. This is called **upcycling**. You get to help our planet and have fun!

GET CREATIVE WITH GIFTS

You can even try upcycling to make gifts for friends and family. Let's make a bottle vase!

Use craft supplies to decorate the bottle.

Markers

Stickers

Glitter

Paint

Remember to put flowers in the vase before giving it as a gift!

FIX AND REUSE

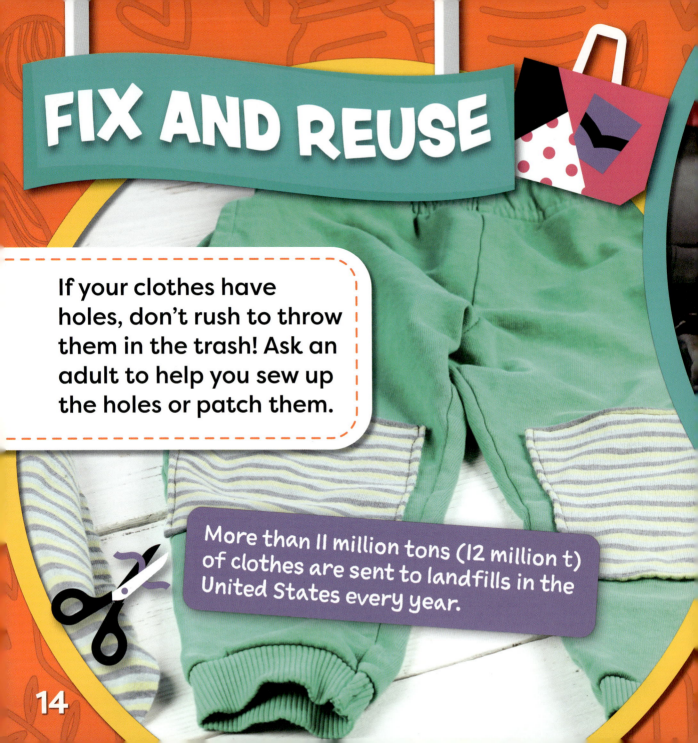

If your clothes have holes, don't rush to throw them in the trash! Ask an adult to help you sew up the holes or patch them.

More than 11 million tons (12 million t) of clothes are sent to landfills in the United States every year.

Fixing clothes to reuse them reduces your waste. You can also buy secondhand clothes. These clothes belonged to someone else before you.

15

DONATE IT

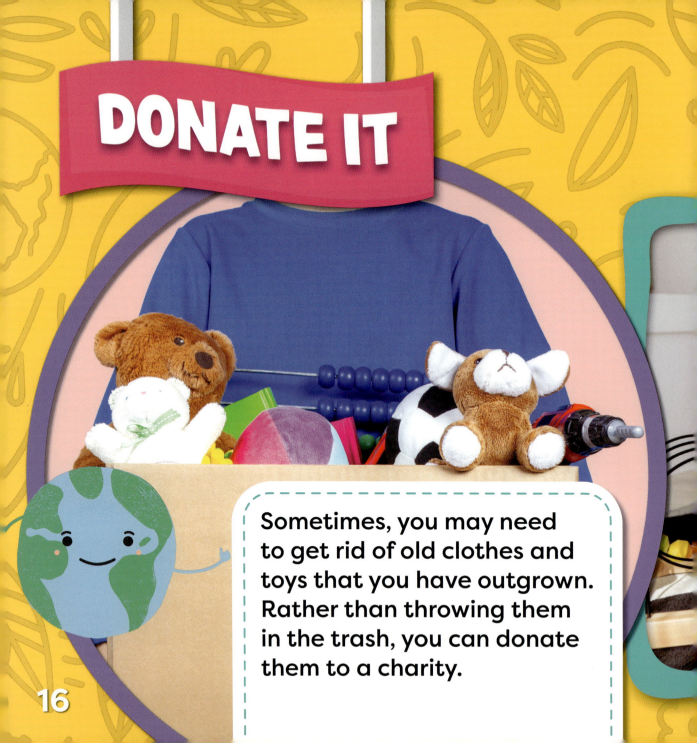

Sometimes, you may need to get rid of old clothes and toys that you have outgrown. Rather than throwing them in the trash, you can donate them to a charity.

When you give clothes and toys to a charity, the items go to people who need them.

A charity may also give food to people or help in other ways.

SAVE ENERGY

Energy is what we use to power many things in our homes. Hot water, television, and lamps all use energy.

Wasting energy is bad for the planet. But here are some ways you can save energy . . .

Turn off lights when you leave a room.

Unplug electronics when you are done using them.

Take shorter showers.

When it is cold, cuddle up with blankets so you can keep the heat turned low.

19

MEAT-FREE MEALS

Big farms that have lots of animals for meat can harm our planet. Eating less meat helps stop that.

Eating even one meat-free meal a week can still help save the planet!

People who don't eat any meat are called **vegetarians**.

COOKING TIME

Veggie wrap

Want to go meat-free but don't know where to start? Try this veggie wrap!

Here's how to make it.

- Gather whatever vegetables you want.
- You could even add some beans or plant-based meat.
- Wrap it all up in a tortilla.

Any food scraps can be turned into **compost**. This helps Earth, too!

GLOSSARY

compost rotted food and other natural things that are added to soil to help plants grow

landfills large holes in the ground used for dumping trash

planet a large, round object that circles the sun

recycle to turn used, unwanted things into new, useful things

reused used again

single-use something that can be used only one time before it must be thrown away or recycled

upcycling making something new from something old

vegetarians people who do not eat meat

INDEX

charity 16–17
clothes 14–17
energy 18–19
landfills 6, 14
recycling 8–9
trash 6, 8, 14, 16
trees 8
upcycling 10–13
vegetarian 21